"I'm going to bed," Mike tells
his dog, Niles.  Niles slides over to
Mike's side to give him a lick.

"Good night!" Mike tells his cat, Stripe. But it isn't time for her to rest. It's time to try to find some nice mice.

2

The nice mice in Mike's house
aren't resting at this time.  They
like to stay up late.

The mice slide down the pipes.
The mice hike and ride little bikes.
The mice fly kites.

Two mice bite a slice of cheese.
Five mice grab nine grapes and a
pack of rice. That's quite a pile!

"If Stripe was here, our fun
would end," whisper the mice.

Tap, tap, tap. It's Stripe!
"It's time to hide," whisper the
wise mice.

Stripe looks for the nice mice.
But the mice are safe in bed.